No Backbone!
The World of Invertebrates

stinging scorpions

by Natalie Lunis

Consultant: Brian V. Brown
Curator, Entomology Section
Natural History Museum of Los Angeles County

BEARPORT
PUBLISHING

NEW YORK, NEW YORK

Credits

Cover, © John Bell/ Shutterstock; TOC, © Rungtip Chatadee/Alamy; 4-5, © X. Eichaker/Bios/Peter Arnold Inc.; 6, © Emanuele Biggi/Oxford Scientific/Photolibrary; 7, © Ray Massey/Photolibrary; 8, © Paul & Joyce Berquist/Animals Animals Enterprises; 9, © Richard Du Toit/Minden Pictures; 10, © Robert & Linda Mitchell; 11, © Robert & Linda Mitchell; 12, © Daniel Heuclin/NHPA/Photoshot; 13, © Michael & Patricia Fogden/Corbis; 14T, © Nigel Dennis/Photolibrary; 14C, © Daniel Heuclin/NHPA/Photoshot; 14B, © D. MacDonald/OSF/Animals Animals Enterprises; 15, © Claro Cortes IV/Reuters/Landov; 16, © Pete Oxford/Nature Picture Library; 17, © Stocksearch/Alamy; 18, © John Bell/Bruce Coleman Inc.; 19, © John Visser/Bruce Coleman Inc.; 20, © Ashok Captain Photographer/Bruce Coleman Inc.; 21, © Robert & Linda Mitchell; 22TL, © Scott T. Slattery/Shutterstock; 22TR, © John Mitchell/OSF/Photolibrary; 22BL, © Scott Camazine/Alamy; 22BR, © Heinrich van den Berg/Gallo Images/Alamy; 22Spot, © Gerrit de Vries/Shutterstock; 23TL, © John Bell/Shutterstock; 23TR, © Jim Wehtje/Photodisc/Getty Images; 23BL, © Ashok Captain Photographer/Bruce Coleman Inc.; 23BR, © Robert & Linda Mitchell; 24, © Ljupco Smokovski/Shutterstock.

Publisher: Kenn Goin
Editorial Director: Adam Siegel
Creative Director: Spencer Brinker
Original Design: Dawn Beard Creative
Photo Researcher: Laura Saravia

Library of Congress Cataloging-in-Publication Data

Lunis, Natalie.
  Stinging scorpions / by Natalie Lunis.
     p. cm. — (No backbone! The world of invertebrates)
  Includes bibliographical references.
  ISBN-13: 978-1-59716-756-7 (library binding)
  ISBN-10: 1-59716-756-8 (library binding)
  1. Scorpions—Juvenile literature. I. Title.

QL458.7.L86 2009
595.4'6—dc22
                              2008042377

For more information, write to Bearport Publishing Company, Inc., 101 Fifth Avenue, Suite 6R, New York, New York 10003. Printed in the United States of America.

10 9 8 7 6 5 4 3 2 1

Contents

Deadly Stingers

Scorpions are small animals with big front claws.

Like spiders, they have eight legs and belong to a group of animals called **arachnids**.

A scorpion, however, has something that no spider has—a tail with a deadly stinger.

Scorpions can be from half an inch (1.3 cm) to 8 inches (20 cm) long.

A Scorpion's Body

Like all arachnids, scorpions have two main body parts—a front part and a back part.

A scorpion's eight legs are attached to the front part, along with a pair of big, powerful claws.

A scorpion uses its claws to grab, tear, and crush other animals.

At the back part of the scorpion's body is its tail.

The tail has a sharp, curved stinger at the end, which can pump poison into the bodies of other animals.

A scorpion also has a hard covering called an exoskeleton on the outside of its body. The exoskeleton protects the scorpion's soft inner body parts and keeps them from drying out.

stinger

tail

legs

claws

7

Warm-Weather Homes

There are about 1,500 kinds of scorpions.

Most live in warm parts of the world.

They live in different kinds of places, including forests, grasslands, and deserts.

The little creatures hide during the day, when the sun is hot.

At night, they come out to hunt insects and other small animals.

About 90 kinds of scorpions live in the United States. Most of them are found in Arizona, Texas, and Oklahoma.

9

Sensing Food

Scorpions have from 2 to 12 eyes, but they do not see well.

They use comb-shaped body parts and hairs to find food.

The combs and hairs feel movements in the ground and in the air.

They tell a scorpion when a victim is coming near.

The combs that a scorpion uses for sensing movement are called **pectines**. They are on the bottom of the scorpion's body, behind its last pair of legs. Scorpions are the only animals in the world that have these special body parts.

pectines (combs)

hairs on tail

11

Tearing into a Meal

When an insect or other animal comes close enough, the scorpion grabs it with its claws.

Often, it tears its victim to pieces and starts to eat right away.

Sometimes, however, the victim is large and puts up a struggle.

When that happens, the scorpion curls its tail over its head and delivers a deadly sting.

Then it digs into its meal.

gecko

Both small and large scorpions eat insects, spiders, worms, and other scorpions. The largest ones also eat lizards, mice, and snakes.

cricket

13

Becoming a Meal

Scorpions have lots of enemies.

Bats and birds swoop down from the air to grab and eat them.

Snakes, lizards, meerkats, and coyotes snatch them on the ground.

When a scorpion can't make a quick getaway, it tries to use its stinger to defend itself.

Still, sometimes an enemy is faster or stronger.

Then the scorpion becomes a meal.

yellow-billed hornbill

desert agama

meerkat

14

fried scorpions
for sale

In China and other
parts of Asia, some
people like to eat
fried scorpions.

A Danger to People?

About 25 kinds of scorpions can kill or badly hurt a person with their sting.

They don't go after people on purpose, but sometimes people come too close to them.

For example, a person can get stung while putting on shoes or clothes.

If a scorpion is hiding in them, it will feel trapped—and sting.

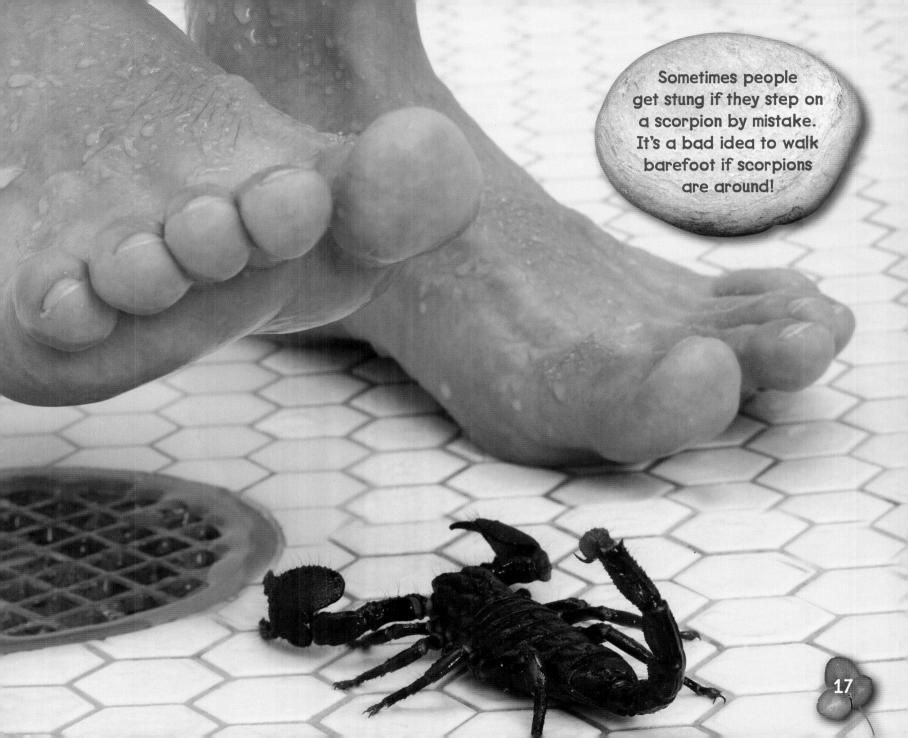

Sometimes people get stung if they step on a scorpion by mistake. It's a bad idea to walk barefoot if scorpions are around!

17

Lots of Babies

Baby scorpions don't hatch from eggs, as other arachnids do.

Instead, they are born alive.

As soon as they come out of their mother's body, they climb onto her back.

The helpless scorpions stay there for two weeks or more while she keeps them safe.

baby scorpions

Scorpions have from 1 to more than 100 babies at a time. Most kinds have about 30 babies.

baby scorpions

On Their Own

While they are still on their mother's back, baby scorpions **molt** for the first time.

They shed the exoskeleton they were born with and form a new, bigger one.

After they climb down and start to live on the ground, they keep getting bigger and stronger.

After four to seven molts, the scorpions are fully grown.

They are ready to live on their own—using their stingers to get food and fight off enemies.

old exoskeleton

Scorpions live from two to ten years.

A World of Invertebrates

An animal that has a skeleton with a **backbone** inside its body is a *vertebrate* (VUR-tuh-brit). Mammals, birds, fish, reptiles, and amphibians are all vertebrates.

An animal that does not have a skeleton with a backbone inside its body is an *invertebrate* (in-VUR-tuh-brit). More than 95 percent of all kinds of animals on Earth are invertebrates.

Some invertebrates, such as insects and spiders, have hard skeletons—called exoskeletons—on the outside of their bodies. Other invertebrates, such as worms and jellyfish, have soft, squishy bodies with no exoskeletons to protect them.

Here are four animals that are related to scorpions. Like scorpions, they are all invertebrates.

Yellow Garden Spider

Goliath Birdeater Tarantula

Deer Tick

Velvet Mite

Glossary

arachnids
(uh-RAK-nidz)
the group of animals that includes scorpions, spiders, and ticks; all arachnids have two main body parts and eight legs

backbone
(BAK-*bohn*)
a group of connected bones that run along the backs of some animals, such as dogs, cats, and fish; also called a spine

molt
(MOHLT)
to shed an old exoskeleton so that a new one can form

old exoskeleton

pectines
(PEK-teenz)
small comb-shaped body parts that a scorpion uses for feeling movement

23

Index

Read More

McFee, Shane. *Scorpions.* New York: Rosen (2008).

Murray, Peter. *Scorpions.* Mankato, MN: The Child's World (2008).

Richardson, Adele D. *Scorpions.* Mankato, MN: Capstone (2003).

Learn More Online

To learn more about scorpions, visit

www.bearportpublishing.com/NoBackbone-CreepyCrawlers

About the Author

Natalie Lunis has written many science and nature books for children. She lives in the Hudson River Valley, just north of New York City.